Trucks Roll!

Trucks Roll!

WORDS BY **George Ella Lyon**

ART BY **Craig Frazier**

Glenview, Illinois ▪ Boston, Massachusetts ▪ Chandler, Arizona ▪
Upper Saddle River, New Jersey

Little Book version of *Trucks Roll!* is published by Pearson.

ISBN 13: 978-0-328-47240-6
ISBN 10:   0-328-47240-9

11 12 13 14 15 V010 18 17 16 15 14

Trucks' wheels
go 'round and 'round.
Trucks' pistons
go up and down.

Trucks roll!

6

Trucks have trailers.
Trucks have cabs.
Some haul rabbits.
Some haul labs.

Some haul apple juice.
Some haul trees.
Water them down
in the desert, please.

Trucks roll!

Trucks bring ice cream.
Trucks bring blocks,
books and bulldozers,
dolls and clocks.

12

Dispatcher calls,
says Get underway!
Chocolate chip cookies
have to travel today.

15

Stacks of puzzles
ready to load.
Spaceships, toy trains—
get them on the road!

Haul them through mountains,
over rivers, past towns—
around blue sky curves,
through rain pounding down.

Trucks roll!

Steering wheel, radio,
horn's deep beep.
TV in the bunk
where tired truckers sleep.

Trucks stop.

23

Stop for traffic lights.
Stop for tolls.
Stop for pork chops
and cinnamon rolls.

Stop for weigh stations.
Stop for gas.
Stop for the night
to let sleepiness pass.

Stars above like headlight beams:
Truckers travel rolling dreams.

Then, key in the slot,
coffee in the cup,
trucker's at the wheel
when the sun comes up.

Trucks roll!